W9-ATY-961

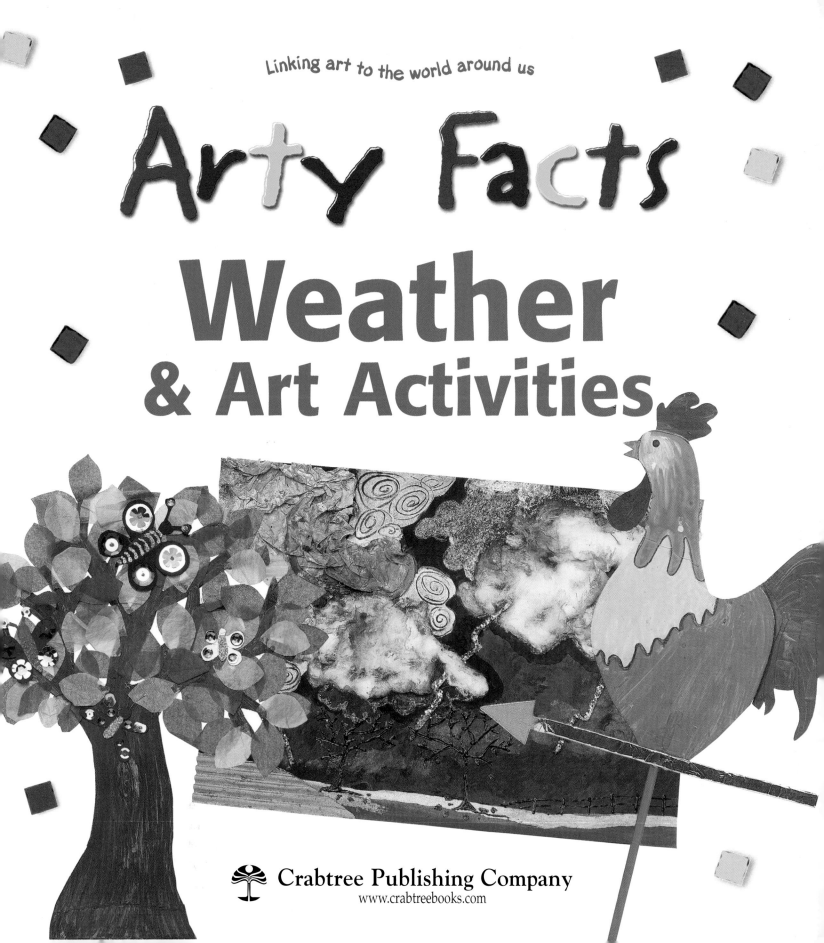

Linking art to the world around us

Arty Facts

Weather
& Art Activities

🌳 Crabtree Publishing Company
www.crabtreebooks.com

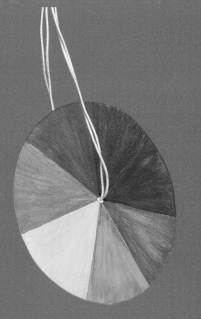

Crabtree Publishing Company

PMB 16A, 350 Fifth Avenue, Suite 3308
New York, NY
10118

612 Welland Avenue
St. Catharines, Ontario
L2M 5V6

Coordinating Editor: Ellen Rodger
Project Editor: Carrie Gleason
Production Coordinator: Rosie Gowsell

Project Development and Concept Marshall Direct:
Editorial Project Director: Karen Foster
Editors: Claire Sippi, Hazel Songhurst, Samantha Sweeney
Researchers: Gerry Bailey, Alec Edgington
Design Director: Tracy Carrington
Designers: Flora Awolaja, Claire Penny, Paul Montague,
James Thompson, Mark Dempsey,
Production: Victoria Grimsell, Christina Brown
Photo Research: Andrea Sadler
Illustrator: Jan Smith
Model Artist: Sophie Dean

Prepress, printing and binding by Worzalla Publishing Company

Sacks, Janet.
    Weather and art activities / written by Janet Sacks.
        p. cm. -- (Arty facts)
    Includes index.
    Summary: Information about various topics related to weather and weather
forecasting forms the foundation for a variety of craft projects.
    ISBN 0-7787-1118-8 (RLB) -- ISBN 0-7787-1146-3 (PB)
    1. Meteorology--Juvenile literature. 2. Weather--Juvenile literature. 3. Weather--
Experiments--Juvenile literature. [1. Meteorology. 2. Weather. 3. Handicraft.] I. Title.
II. Series.
        QC863.5 .S33 2003
        551.5--dc21

                                                        2002011633
                                                        LC

Created by
Marshall Direct Learning
© 2002 Marshall Direct Learning

All rights reserved. No part of this publication may be reproduced, stored in a retrieval
system, or transmitted, in any form or by any means, electronic, mechanical,
photocopying, recording or otherwise, without prior written permission from the
publisher.

FRONT COVER IMAGES: TREVOR MEIN/ TONY STONE IMAGES; ROBERT HARDING PICTURE LIBRARY;

Linking art to the world around us

Arty Facts

Weather

& Art Activities

Contents

WRITTEN BY Janet Sacks

Weather watch

DIGITAL VISION

Have you ever taken shelter in a doorway, knowing that the downpour will be over in a few minutes? Or looked at the sky to see whether it is cloudy or clear? If so, you are a weather forecaster, without realizing it!

Cloud clues

People have always forecast the weather, even before they had scientific equipment to help them. Instead, they looked at weather patterns. **Clouds** give a clue to future weather. A thin, ripply cloud means good weather is on the way. A dark gray, low cloud is a sign of rain. The sky's color is another clue: deep-blue means the air holds only a little water vapor, reddish-colored skies means it holds a bit more, and pearly gray means that it contains a lot. If you get to know the weather patterns in your area, you will be able to forecast the weather yourself!

Modern forecasts

Today, accurate **weather forecasts** are broadcast around the world, up to five days in advance. Farmers listen to television or radio weather forecasts to help them decide when to plant or to harvest their crops. Pilots need to know the local weather conditions before flying their planes. Sailors at sea listen to weather forecasts to find out how strong the **winds** are on the seas.

Changing weather

Wherever you go on Earth, you encounter weather. And no matter where you are, the weather is always changing. The biggest changes happen as the seasons change throughout the year. Each season has its own weather, from hurricanes and monsoons to blizzards and droughts.

Weather

Keep a colorful weekly weather report

WHAT YOU NEED

pencil

poster board

glitter

paintbrush

ruler

glue

paints

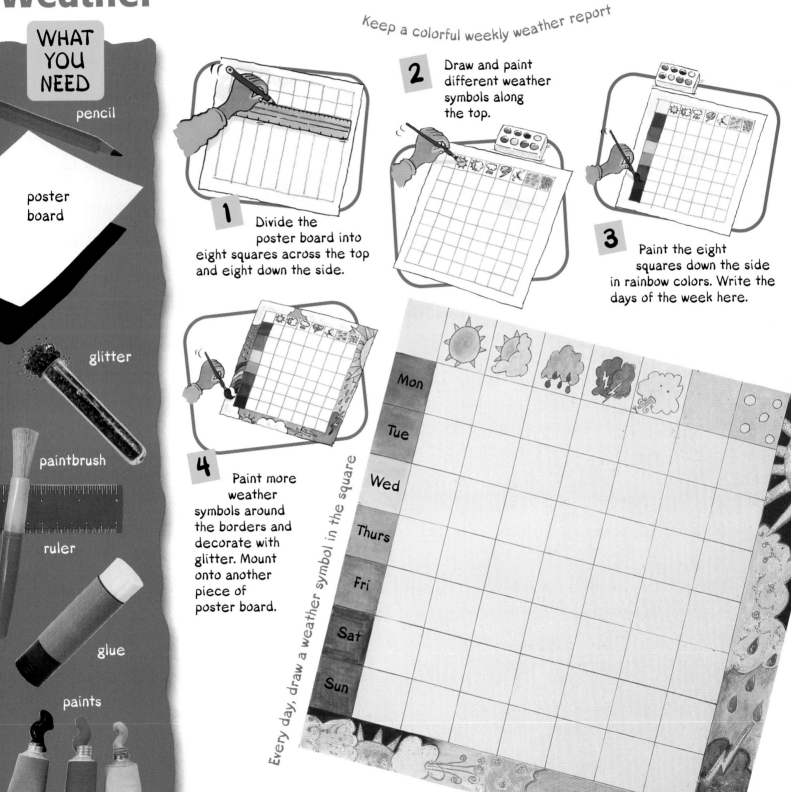

1 Divide the poster board into eight squares across the top and eight down the side.

2 Draw and paint different weather symbols along the top.

3 Paint the eight squares down the side in rainbow colors. Write the days of the week here.

4 Paint more weather symbols around the borders and decorate with glitter. Mount onto another piece of poster board.

Every day, draw a weather symbol in the square

Mon
Tue
Wed
Thurs
Fri
Sat
Sun

5

Rainmakers

When you look up at the sky, you are likely to see the gray or white shapes of clouds. Sometimes, they are puffy and white, dotting the sky here and there. At other times, they cover the sky in a dull, gray sheet. There are many different types of clouds, formed by different types of weather. If you look out the same window every day for a week, you will see several kinds of clouds. Four common cloud types are fluffy **cumulus**, streaky **cirrus**, faint streaks of **stratus**, and **cumulonimbus** storm clouds.

How clouds are made

Clouds form and then disappear in a continuous cycle as water rises into the air from the surface of the Earth and falls back down. When **rain** falls it collects in rivers, lakes and oceans. The heat of the Sun warms the water, causing it to **evaporate** and rise as a gas called **water vapor**.

It's raining

As water vapor rises higher into the **atmosphere**, **air pressure** and **temperature** fall. This condenses, or changes, the water vapor into droplets which form clouds. The droplets then begin to gather together around specks of dust carried by the wind. Gradually, the droplets get bigger. When they are too heavy to float in the air, they fall to the ground again as rain.

TONY STONE IMAGES

Weather

Fluffy cloud pictures

Create a storm and fill the sky with fabric and spatter clouds

WHAT YOU NEED

cotton balls

scissors

sponge

glue

colored paper

toothbrush

pieces of fabric

white paint

1 Cut pieces of fabric into cloud shapes.

2 Glue them onto a piece of colored paper.

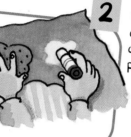

3

Create different shapes from the cotton balls and add these to your fluffy cloud picture.

fabric clouds

spatter clouds

Spatter effect clouds

1 Mix some thick white powdered paint.

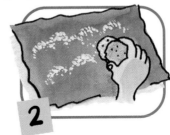

2 Print different cloud shapes on colored paper using the sponge dipped in paint.

3 Use the toothbrush to spatter paint and create light, see-through clouds.

Blowing winds

ADAM WOOLFITT/ CORBIS

Wind is air moving across the Earth. It may be a pleasant, gentle breeze, or strong enough to knock you off your feet. Some winds can be dangerous. A **gale** can whip up large ocean waves that damage ships and flood land. A hurricane can destroy buildings and blow cars off roads.

Weather changer

The direction and strength of the wind affects our **climate** and weather. A wind blowing from a cool, dry area to a warmer, wet area might cause the temperature and amount of moisture in the air to fall suddenly. Clouds, rain, and even **lightning** may occur where the two **air masses** meet. Later, a wind bringing warm air may cause rain showers and a rise in temperature.

Hot air, cold air

Winds are created when the air around the Earth is unevenly heated by the Sun. The hotter air becomes lighter and rises. Cooler air then rushes in to take its place. The cooler air is then warmed, rises, and is replaced by another rush of cool air. Where this circulation of air occurs almost all the time, strong winds called **prevailing winds** blow. Prevailing winds include the **trade winds** that blow east to west across the oceans.

Naming the wind

Most winds are known by the direction they blow from. Others have special names. The mistral blows southward in France. A chinook blows westward over the Rocky Mountains in Canada.

Weather

Spinning weathervane

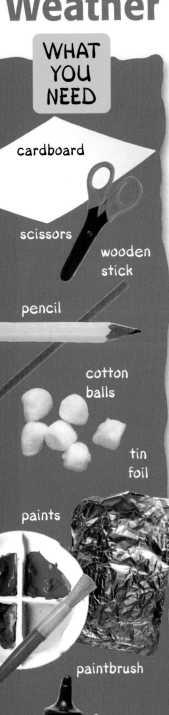

WHAT YOU NEED

cardboard

scissors

wooden stick

pencil

cotton balls

tin foil

paints

paintbrush

glue

straw

Can you see which way the wind is blowing?

1 Sketch the outline of a rooster on the cardboard. Cut it out and paint both sides.

2 Draw and cut out an arrow shape and cover it with silver foil.

3 Glue the arrow to the bottom of your rooster.

4 Glue a straw to the bottom of the rooster and plug the top end with a cotton ball.

Place a thin stick inside the straw. Push the stick into the ground. Now the weathervane can spin in the wind!

5

9

Scattered showers

The water in a raindrop has fallen to Earth many times. Every day, the Sun dries up vast amounts of water from seas, lakes, rivers, plant leaves, puddles, and even from your breath. The water rises into the air and forms clouds, then falls again as rain.

A recycling cycle

The **water cycle** is a system that allows Earth's water to be used over and over again. This is how it works: the Sun's heat evaporates, or changes the water on Earth into a gas called water vapor. The water vapor collects and floats higher and higher until it reaches cooler air. The coolness of the air changes the vapor from a gas back into tiny droplets of water, which join to make a cloud.

Rain or drizzle?

At first, the water droplets in the cloud are so small and light that they float. As the **air currents** move them around, they join to form bigger, heavier drops. Finally, the drops fall as rain. Scientists call water droplets more than one-fiftieth of an inch (0.5 mm) wide, rain. Smaller droplets falling close together are called drizzle. It is easy to tell rain from drizzle. When a raindrop falls into a puddle, it makes a splash!

Measuring the level

Scientists measure rain by catching the raindrops in a rain gauge. A rain gauge has a scale on it that measures the level of the water after one hour of rainfall. Less than one-fiftieth of an inch (0.5 mm) of rain is called light rainfall. A medium rainfall is between one-fiftieth and one-sixth of an inch (0.5 and 4 mm), and heavy rainfall is more than one-sixth of an inch (4 mm).

Rainfall roundup

It rains more in some parts of the world than in others. In a dry, hot desert, rain may hardly ever fall. In warm, tropical countries, such as India, over 4,000 inches (10,000 cm) of rain can fall in one year!

LEE FROST/ ROBERT HARDING PICTURE LIBRARY

Weather

Drip paintings

WHAT
YOU
NEED

paper

poster
board

paints
and
brush

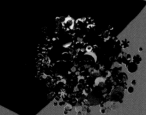

colored
acetate

sequins

glue

1 Water down some colored paint and brush across the top of the paper.

2 Hold the paper upright and let the paint run down.

Next time it rains have fun making rainy day pictures!

4 Glue the shapes onto your picture and decorate with sequins.

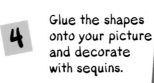

3 Draw and paint some people or animal shapes and cut them out.

5 Cut out umbrella shapes from the acetate and glue onto your picture.

Whiteout

S nowstorms can be fun, but heavy snow with high winds can also be frightening, and sometimes dangerous. This kind of snowstorm is called a blizzard, and it often creates a **whiteout**, in which nothing can be seen except a vast curtain of white.

Blowing blizzards

A blizzard occurs when a cold air mass from the **Arctic region** drifts south into the warmer, temperate regions of the world. When the two air masses meet, the colder, heavier air forces the warmer, lighter air to rise. This leads to a blizzard.

Swirling flakes

In a blizzard, snow falls heavily and the wind blows at 35 miles per hour (56 km/h) or more. The temperature drops to 10°F (−12°C) or colder. The distance you can see, called the range of visibility, is reduced to under 500 feet (150 m). In a severe blizzard, there may be winds of up to 45 miles per hour (72 km/h). At the same time, visibility can drop almost to zero, creating a total whiteout.

Snowdrift zones

Blizzards happen most often across the northern United States, much of Canada, Russia, northern Europe, and northern Asia. The results are heavy, drifting snow, which causes major problems on roads and in towns.

MICHAEL S.YAMASHITA/ CORBIS

Snowflake collage

Cover your window with pretty snowflake patterns

WHAT YOU NEED

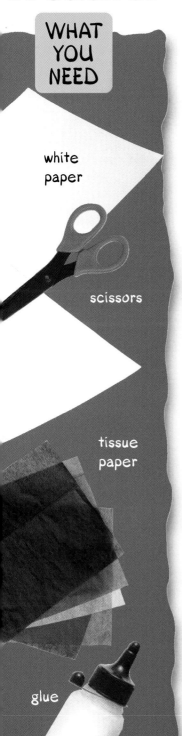

white paper

scissors

tissue paper

glue

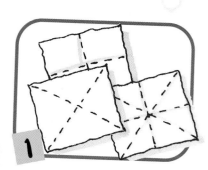

1 Fold square pieces of paper in a variety of ways to create different patterns.

2 Cut out shapes from each folded piece of paper.

3 Unfold each piece of paper and smooth them out flat.

4 Glue your snowflakes on to some tissue paper.

13

Thunderclap

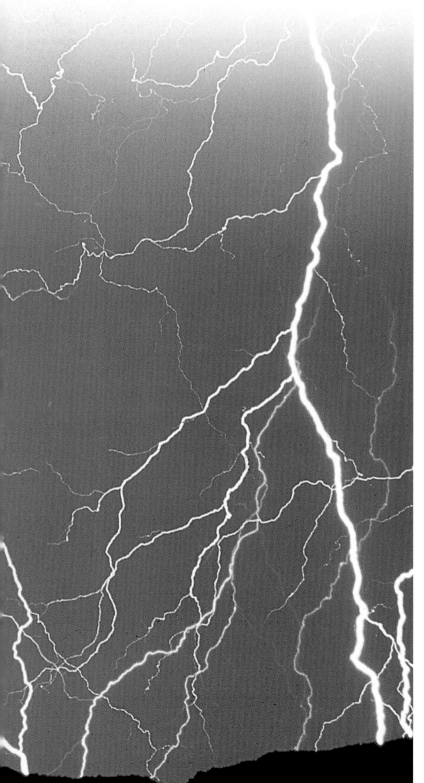

Have you ever watched a thunderstorm from your window? It is exciting and scary at the same time! Lightning suddenly zig-zags across the sky in a gigantic flash. It is quickly followed by a deep, rumbling sound and a loud crash of **thunder**! What causes it?

Electric charge

Lightning happens when electricity builds up in a rain cloud. Each water drop in the cloud has a tiny charge of electricity. There are billions of water drops, so the whole cloud has a powerful charge of electricity. When the cloud comes close to another cloud with an **electric charge**, or to the ground, electricity rushes between them. The lightning flash we see is a large electric spark. Each flash may be 20 miles (30 km) long and last about 0.2 seconds!

Lightning strikes

Lightning always finds the fastest way to the ground, usually through a tall tree or a building. It is very unusual for a person to be struck by lightning, but you should never shelter under a tree during a thunderstorm. If the height of the tree attracts the lightning, it might strike you!

Thunder roll

Lightning heats up the air it flashes through, causing an explosion that sends out **shock waves** in all directions. It is these shock waves that we hear as thunder.

ROBERT HARDING PICTURE LIBRARY

Weather

Stormscape

Create a dramatic stormy picture with lightning flashes!

WHAT YOU NEED

cotton balls

paper

tissue paper

poster board

silver foil

paints and brush

glitter

pipe cleaners glue

silver paint

1 Glue clouds made from cotton balls, scrunched up tissue paper, and silver foil onto the paper.

2

Paint all over with silver and sprinkle with glitter.

3 Glue glitter onto pipe cleaners. Shape them into lightning forks and glue onto the picture.

4 Paint a landscape with trees. Decorate the leaves with glitter.

5 Mount on a piece of poster board.

Make your picture shine with silver and gold

Sky bridges

NICK WOOD/ ROBERT HARDING PICTURE LIBRARY

A fter it has rained, you sometimes see a beautiful **rainbow** arching across the sky. Long ago, people believed rainbows were magical and invented all kinds of stories about them. The real magic of a multi-colored rainbow is that it is made of pure, **white light**!

White light

White light is a mixture of all the colors we see in a rainbow! Light travels in different sized **light waves**, called wavelengths. Each color has a different wavelength. Red, for example, has a longer wavelength than violet.

Bending sunlight

Light bends as it moves from thin air to thicker water. This is why a straight stick in a glass of water looks partly bent. After a rainfall, the air is still full of water. The water in the air causes the sunlight to bend, splitting it into colors that form a rainbow. Just as white light can be split into different colors, they can be mixed up to make white again.

Color count

The colors that make white light are called the colors of the **spectrum**. In a rainbow, you will always see these colors in the same order: red, orange, yellow, green, blue, indigo, violet. A second rainbow reverses the order so that violet is at the top.

Weather

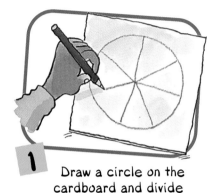

WHAT YOU NEED

cardboard

scissors

paints and brush

needle

pencil

ruler

rubber band

Rainbow spinner

1 Draw a circle on the cardboard and divide it into seven sections.

2 Paint the seven colors of the rainbow, one in each section.

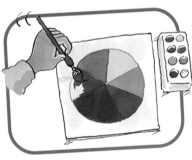

3 Cut the circle out and paint the other side exactly the same.

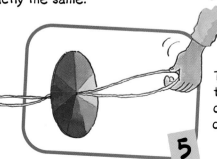

4 Make a hole in the middle of the circle.

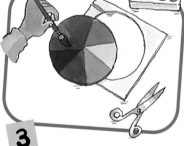

5 Thread a rubber band through the center. Twist it to make the circle spin fast. Now watch the colors blend into white.

Spin the rainbow spinner and watch the colors merge to white

17

Frosted patterns

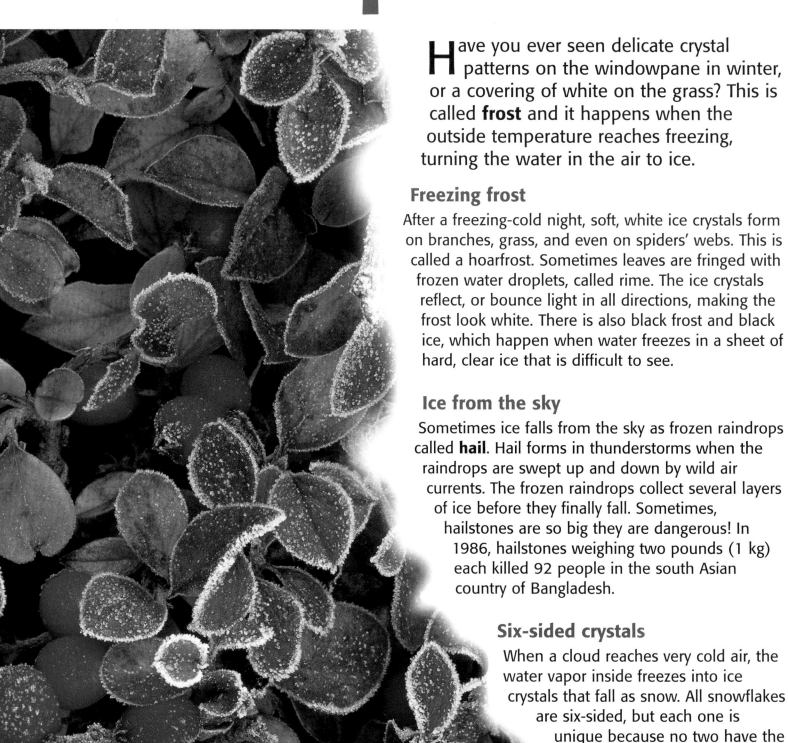

Have you ever seen delicate crystal patterns on the windowpane in winter, or a covering of white on the grass? This is called **frost** and it happens when the outside temperature reaches freezing, turning the water in the air to ice.

Freezing frost

After a freezing-cold night, soft, white ice crystals form on branches, grass, and even on spiders' webs. This is called a hoarfrost. Sometimes leaves are fringed with frozen water droplets, called rime. The ice crystals reflect, or bounce light in all directions, making the frost look white. There is also black frost and black ice, which happen when water freezes in a sheet of hard, clear ice that is difficult to see.

Ice from the sky

Sometimes ice falls from the sky as frozen raindrops called **hail**. Hail forms in thunderstorms when the raindrops are swept up and down by wild air currents. The frozen raindrops collect several layers of ice before they finally fall. Sometimes, hailstones are so big they are dangerous! In 1986, hailstones weighing two pounds (1 kg) each killed 92 people in the south Asian country of Bangladesh.

Six-sided crystals

When a cloud reaches very cold air, the water vapor inside freezes into ice crystals that fall as snow. All snowflakes are six-sided, but each one is unique because no two have the same pattern!

PHIL MCLEAN/ HOLT STUDIOS

Weather

Add some birds, animals or even a snowman to your picture

WHAT YOU NEED

silver foil

newspaper

glitter

glue

sequins

shells

strips of bubble wrap

twigs

colored poster board

pebbles

string

1 Glue strips of newspaper and bubble wrap across a sheet of silver foil.

2 Glue small twigs, pebbles, and shells onto the picture and decorate it with glitter.

3 Glue string pieces to the sky as shown, and add sequins for snowflakes.

Mount onto poster board.

4

19

The big sleep

Winter sleep

As cold weather approaches, food supplies decrease. When it is cold, animals need more food to stay warm and give them energy, so some hibernate, or go to sleep. A hibernating mammal lowers its body temperature from around 90°F (32°C) to 40°F (4°C). Its heart and breathing also slow down. This way, the body uses hardly any energy to stay alive. For example, a hibernating hedgehog may only breathe once every six minutes! Animals get ready to hibernate by gorging on food in the autumn. When they wake again in spring, they may have lost nearly half their body weight.

Hiding place

All hibernating animals have to find a safe, warm place for their winter sleep. Some animals, such as mice, **burrow** underground. Bats hang upside down in hollow trees or a warm barn. Snails squeeze into cracks or under rocks, and seal the entrance to their shell with a thin skin called a membrane. Some animals do not hide away for long. On mild winter days, squirrels and bears wake up and search for food.

A long, hot summer

In hot climates, some animals hibernate through a **drought**. This is called estivation. Although male Californian ground squirrels sleep, the females must stay awake to look after their young. The African lungfish gorges itself on food during the rainy season, then burrows into the mud during periods of drought.

As the weather turns colder and winter comes, some animals seem to disappear. We do not see bats flying at night, or snakes slithering through the grass because these animals spend the winter in a deep sleep.

R.P.LAWRENCE/ FLPA

Weather

WHAT YOU NEED

- dried leaves
- newspaper
- tissue paper
- paints and brush
- hay
- cardboard box
- scissors
- glitter
- poster board
- paper
- pencil
- glue

Hibernation box

1 Cut an opening on one side of the box. Make a hill shape on top with scrunched-up newspaper, and glue it on. Paint the hill green or brown when dry.

2 Cut leaf shapes out of tissue paper and glue them all over the box. Add some real dry leaves. Put hay or grass inside.

Make a model of a hibernating animal to put into your box

Animal windows

Draw a tree landscape on a piece of paper. Paint and decorate with glitter. Cut little window shapes from the leaves and trunks.

1

2 Draw and paint some hibernating animals and cut them out.

3 Position the animals to line up with the holes you cut on the trees. Glue them onto colored poster board. Now put your nature scene on top.

Turn the picture over and open the windows of your nature scene

Weather machines

PETER MENZEL/ SCIENCE PHOTO LIBRARY

No one knows exactly how hot, cold, or wet it will be tomorrow or next week. The weather can change so quickly that even the experts get it wrong! To help them make their forecasts, scientists collect information using different weather instruments.

On the surface

Some instruments gather information from near the Earth's surface. A **barometer** measures air pressure. A reading of "High" usually means clear, sunny skies, and "Low" means cloud or rain. An anemometer measures wind speed, and a hygrometer measures the **humidity**, or amount of water in the air.

Weather balloons

Every day, **weather balloons** are sent high into the air. They carry measuring instruments to record air temperature, humidity, and wind speed. The information is sent back to **weather stations** on the ground.

Space spies

Weather satellites are launched into space. They send pictures of the weather around the world back to computers on Earth. But the satellite pictures are not like pictures from an ordinary camera. One type of picture measures temperature. It shows the heat coming from the Earth's surface, the clouds, oceans and air, as different colors.

Weather

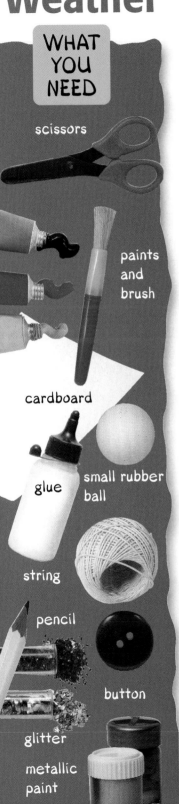

WHAT YOU NEED

scissors

paints and brush

cardboard

glue

small rubber ball

string

pencil

button

glitter

metallic paint

Ping-pong hail ball

How many times can you bat the ball before you miss it?

Draw and cut out a paddle shape from cardboard.

1

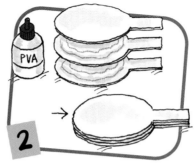

2

Cut out several more paddles then glue at least three together for strength. Paint and decorate with glitter.

3

Thread string through the center of the paddle and attach to the rubber ball.

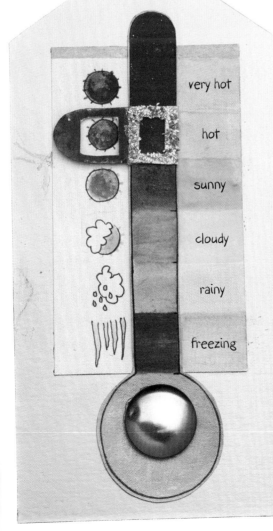

very hot

hot

sunny

cloudy

rainy

freezing

Barometer

1. Draw a thermometer shape on white cardboard. Cut it out.

2. Paint blocks of color on the thermometer from blue at the bottom to red at the top.

3. Make a tab by folding a small strip of cardboard into two. Cut two windows from the tab. Glue the ends together, leaving a gap so one window can slip over the thermometer.

4. Glue the thermometer shape onto cardboard. Add a silver-painted button. Decorate the cardboard with weather symbols.

5. Cut a hole in the top of the cardboard so you can hang your barometer up.

Halos and glories

An illusion

In hot weather, you sometimes think you see pools of water on a dry road. This is an **optical illusion**, caused by bending light. The air close to the road heats up and spreads. Light entering this hot, thin air is bent. You see a brightness, which is actually a **reflection** of the sky above.

Trick of the light

Sailors in polar regions have sometimes seen mountains floating on the sea! This is caused by colder, thicker air lying just above the sea's surface. When light rays pass through this thicker air, images of far away mountains are reflected onto the water. Even stranger, the layer of warmer air above the cold air can twist the light rays – turning the mountains upside down! Often large ships first see one another as an upside-down picture in the sky!

Ghostly halos

When there is a lot of thin cloud in the sky, a ghostly white **halo** with a red rim can appear around the moon. It is formed in the same way as a rainbow, only the light is bent by ice crystals in the air, instead of raindrops.

HEATHER ANGEL

L ight can play tricks on us. Sometimes, it causes us to see things that are not there. People claim to have seen water in the desert or to have counted nine suns! This is because light bends as it travels through the sky.

Glories

When clouds are low in the sky, it is possible to see the shadow of an airplane flying above them. The shadow may have rings of colored light, called glories, all around it. Glories are caused when light enters the edge of water droplets and bounces back. The light rays cross over, either destroying or joining each other.

Weather

WHAT
YOU
NEED

white
paper

glue

paints and brush

water

colored
poster board

1 Paint the piece of paper with water.

2 Dot blobs of color on the wet paper and watch them spread out.

3 When dry, mount your halo pictures on colored poster board.

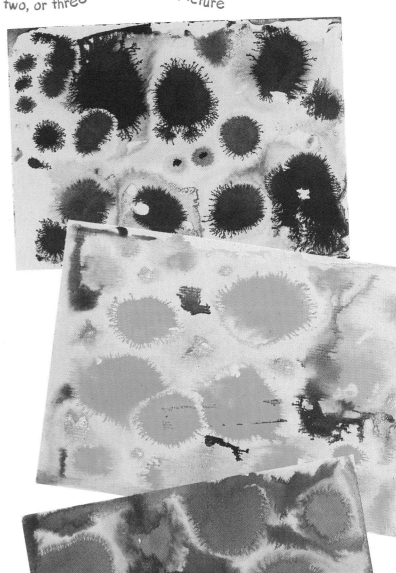

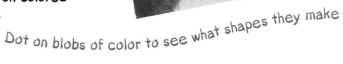

Dot on blobs of color to see what shapes they make

Earth's blanket

The atmosphere is the layer of gases around the Earth that we call the air. It is like a blanket, keeping the world warm and protecting it from the Sun's more harmful rays. Unfortunately, the atmosphere is under attack from pollution and only we can help it.

Dangerous hole

In the 1980s, scientists found a hole in the **ozone layer** of the atmosphere. This layer stops the Sun's dangerous, **ultraviolet rays** reaching the Earth. The ozone layer was being destroyed by chemicals called **CFC**s that were used in foam packing, refrigerators, and spray bottles. Most countries have now banned CFCs, but the damage they have caused might last for many years.

The greenhouse effect

The lower part of the atmosphere contains the gases that keep heat close to the Earth. These gases are called greenhouse gases because they work like the glass in a greenhouse. They let in light, but they do not let out heat. Without the greenhouse effect, the Earth would be cold and frozen. The problem is that pollution in the atmosphere has made the Earth heat up more than normal. Even a small rise in temperature can change the world's climate, leading to unusual weather, rising sea levels, and serious floods.

Carbon dioxide

The main greenhouse gas is carbon dioxide. There is more in the atmosphere today than ever before. Carbon dioxide comes from car exhaust and from burning coal, gas, and oil in **power stations**. It is also produced when a rainforest is cleared by burning. To lower carbon dioxide levels, we must burn less fossil fuel, clear fewer rainforests, and use cleaner car fuel.

Weather

WHAT YOU NEED

cardboard box

paper fasteners

tissue paper

tape

scissors

pipe cleaners

cellophane

small plants

paints and brush

Mini greenhouse

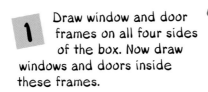

1 Draw window and door frames on all four sides of the box. Now draw windows and doors inside these frames.

2 Cut out the windows and doors. Do not cut out the frames. Paint the framework and floor green.

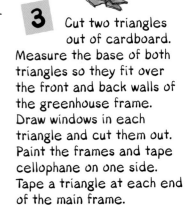

3 Cut two triangles out of cardboard. Measure the base of both triangles so they fit over the front and back walls of the greenhouse frame. Draw windows in each triangle and cut them out. Paint the frames and tape cellophane on one side. Tape a triangle at each end of the main frame.

4 Fold another piece of cardboard in half and cut it to size so that it opens to make a roof. Cut out windows, paint the frames, and tape cellophane on one side.

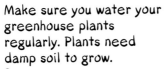

Make sure you water your greenhouse plants regularly. Plants need damp soil to grow.

Make climbing flowers from twisted pipe cleaners and tissue paper

Cracked earth

Imagine turning on the tap and no water runs out. You cannot have a drink when you feel thirsty, or a shower to wash. You might think this is okay – for a little while. But when a country runs out of water for a long time, the problems can be very serious.

No rain

When rain that is expected does not come, it is called a drought. The drought might only last a short time, but sometimes a drought can last for months, or even years.

Dried up

A drought affects people's lives because there is not enough water for everything. When the water supply begins to be used up, it may have to be carefully rationed, or shared. Farmers may not be able to water their crops, sheep and cattle may not have enough grass to eat because it has dried up, and fish may die because the water level in lakes and rivers drops too low.

Deadly drought

In 1968, a drought began in a narrow area of land called the Sahel, running across Africa on the edge of the Sahara desert. In some parts of Africa, the drought is still going on. In 1983, drought hit Ethiopia in the north-east of Africa. Without rain, crops could not grow. The country soon ran out of food and thousands of people began to walk south. When they reached the Sudan, they faced more hunger because there was a drought there the next year.

ROGER TIDMAN/ FLPA

Weather

Deadly desert scene

Picture the sun beating down on the dry desert sands

WHAT YOU NEED

yellow and blue poster board

white paint

paints and brush

glue

pencil

white poster board

scissors

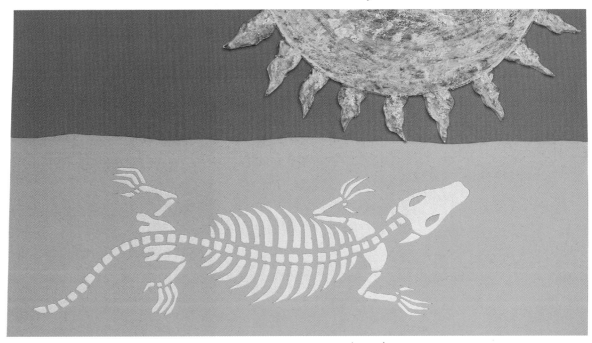

Create a split-level scene from colored poster board

1 Using a very sharp pencil, draw a skeleton on yellow poster board. You can trace over the picture above, or draw a shape of your own.

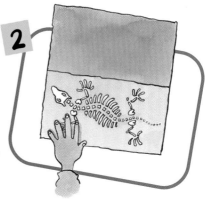

2 With white paint, color the individual bones of your skeleton very carefully. Then stick a sheet of blue poster board above the yellow poster board, as shown.

3 Paint and decorate half a sun shape on poster board and cut it out.

4 Glue the sun onto your desert picture.

29

Green oasis

ROBERT HARDING PICTURE LIBRARY

A desert is a dry, bare place where it hardly ever rains and where few plants can grow. Sometimes a green patch of land suddenly appears, full of growing plants and fresh water. This fertile spot is called an oasis.

Hot and cold

Deserts are so far away from the sea that the winds that blow there have lost their moisture. Most deserts are hot places, but there are some cold deserts. Cold deserts are usually flat stretches of land high in the mountains. They are scorching hot in summer and freezing cold in winter.

Mountain water

An oasis appears where underground water comes to the surface. This water falls first as rain or snow on a faraway hill or mountain. It soaks into the ground and trickles through underground rocks to a low place in the desert. Then it flows up through a crack in the rock.

Fertile land

With a supply of water all year, plants grow well on the desert soil. People have settled near large oases, and have even built cities. There they can grow wheat and fruit as well as clover to feed their sheep and camels.

Weather

Palm tree paradise

WHAT YOU NEED

cardboard box lid

tissue paper

double-sided tape

pencil

sand

scissors

cardboard

glue

green glitter

paints and brush

1 Glue and sprinkle sand to cover the inside of the box lid. Cut a circle out of tissue paper and decorate with glitter to make a pool of water.

Draw the tops of palm trees and trunks on cardboard as shown. Paint and decorate with glitter. Cut out when dry.

2

3

Bring the two ends of the treetops together. Attach with double-sided tape so they curve downward.

4 Fold the trunks in half and tape together. Attach to the palms.

5 Draw bushes and grass on cardboard. Cut out and decorate.

6 Make slits so you can slot the pieces of grass and bushes together as shown. Glue everything to the base to complete your oasis.

Arrange all your plants around the pool in your shimmering oasis

Solar panels

The mirrors on this solar station are computer-controlled to track the path of the Sun.

PETER MENZEL/ SCIENCE PHOTO LIBRARY

We call the heat and warmth from the Sun **solar energy**. More of this energy reaches Earth than can ever be made in our millions of power stations. There are many ways to collect and use this amazing sun power.

Hot house

A solar house is a house heated by the sun. It has special collectors called **solar panels** built on the roof or on the sunniest side of the house. Water flows through pipes inside the solar panels. During the day, this water is heated by the sunlight and pumped around the house.

Heat makes power

In the hot Mojave desert in southern California, a curved mirror reflects sunlight onto an enormous pipe filled with water. The water heats up and boils to make steam. The steam power turns a motor, called a **turbine**, to make electricity. In France, a solar furnace, or oven, is heated by hundreds of small mirrors reflecting sunlight onto one gigantic mirror. The Sun's energy is reflected off the mirror toward the furnace.

Solar cells

Solar cells are made of a material that makes electricity when light shines on it. Some cells work in ordinary indoor light, as well as natural sunlight. Many calculators and watches have solar cells. A group of large solar cells can make enough electricity for several homes, making solar power useful for small villages far from electricity supplies. There are even cars fitted with solar cells to power an electric motor.

Weather

Sun home

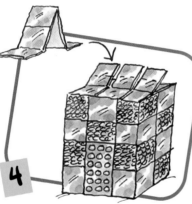

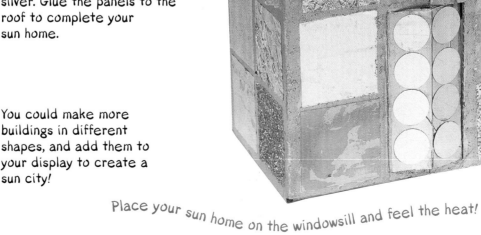

WHAT YOU NEED

cardboard box

glue

large sequins

scissors

bubble wrap

silver paint

silver foil

1 Paint the box silver.

2 Cut out square windows from bubble wrap and foil, and glue onto all four sides of the box.

3 Cut out a door from the front of the box, and glue on sequins.

4 Fold long rectangles of cardboard into a V shape with small panels on each side, as shown above. Paint them silver. Glue the panels to the roof to complete your sun home.

You could make more buildings in different shapes, and add them to your display to create a sun city!

Place your sun home on the windowsill and feel the heat!

33

Weird weather

Have you ever heard anyone say it is "raining cats and dogs" when there is a downpour? It could never really rain cats or dogs – or could it? There are stories of objects and animals falling from the sky.

Toad storm

A tornado, or whirlwind, is a whirling funnel of wind. A really powerful tornado can spin so fast it can pick up a heavy truck or uproot a tree. A weaker wind, sweeping across a pond full of frogs, could easily lift them into the air, carry them along and then drop them far away. This was the explanation for a rainstorm of toads that fell over a town in Mexico in 1997!

Raining fish

A **waterspout** traveling across a lake or the sea can suck up the fish and dump them on the land. In the European country of Norway, a powerful waterspout once emptied a small harbor of all its fish – and all its water!

Rainbow snow

A rainstorm sometimes leaves behind streaks of dirt or grains of sand. Sand from a faraway, warm desert can be carried thousands of miles by the wind. When the wind reaches a cooler place, the sand falls to the ground in rain. Snow falling in the Alps mountains in Europe is sometimes colored pink, red, or brown by sand from the Sahara desert in Africa, 1,245 miles (2,000 km) away!

Duck for dinner!

Some weather tales really make you wonder! Try to explain these old stories: a downpour of large, yellow mice; a heavy shower of black eggs; a terrifying fall of live snakes! The funniest of all was in 1973, in Arkansas, when frozen ducks dropped out of the sky. Now, how do you think that happened?

RICHARD BROOKS/ FLPA

Weather

It's raining frogs and fish

WHAT YOU NEED

paper

poster board

glue

sequins

glitter

paints and brush

pencil

scissors

white wax crayon

1 Rub the white wax crayon all over the paper, then add a wash of blue paint on top.

2 Draw and paint many different fish and frogs on a separate piece of paper.

3 Cut out the shapes and glue them onto the paper.

Wax and paint mix to produce an excellent 'water' effect

4 Decorate with glitter and sequins.

5 Mount on poster board. You can cover your painting with waterproof cellophane and hang it up in the bathroom!

35

Washed up

All around the world, people have built towns and villages by rivers. A river supplies water for homes, farms, and factories. The river can also carry people and goods from place to place. There is just one problem living so close to a river – flooding.

An overflow

A flood happens when a river swells with too much water. If nothing stops it, a river can burst its banks and send water rushing into homes, businesses, and across farmers' fields. The Yangtze river in China has flooded out of control like this many times. For thousands of years, farmers in Egypt have welcomed the yearly Nile river floods because it fertilizes the soil.

Rain and ice

A flood can happen when a lot of rain falls in a short time. When winds full of moisture blow overland to Asia from the Indian Ocean, they bring heavy rain and flooding which can last for months! This is called the monsoon. The Danube river in Europe often floods in spring, when ice breaks away from its banks and piles up, causing an overflow.

Flood control

There are ways to slow down or even stop flooding. Riverbanks can be built up with earth, rock, or concrete to create a wall that the water cannot pass through. A concrete dam can hold back the water and a barrier across a river can be lowered to slow the speed of the water.

BRIAN BRAKE/ SCIENCE PHOTO LIBRARY

Weather

All-weather hats

WHAT YOU NEED

poster board

sequins

scissors   glue

paints and brush

varnish

rubber band

pencil

tape

tissue paper

1 Cut a circle out of poster board. Then cut a line from the edge to the middle.

2 Overlap the edges into a cone shape and glue them together.

PVA

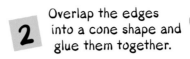

3 Paint and decorate your hat. Tape a piece of rubber band to make a strap under your chin. Varnish to waterproof.

Rainhat

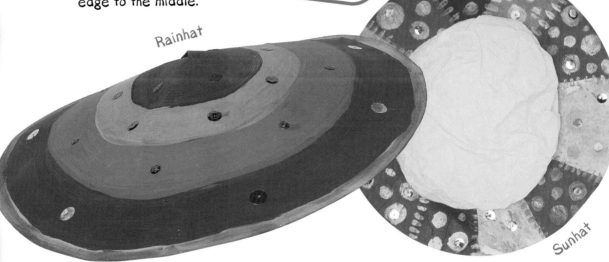

Sunhat

---

1 Draw and cut a circle from the poster board and cut out a smaller circle inside the big one.

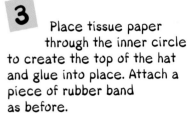

PVA

3 Place tissue paper through the inner circle to create the top of the hat and glue into place. Attach a piece of rubber band as before.

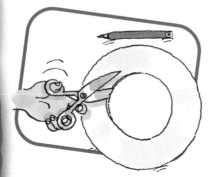

2 Paint and decorate the larger circle with sequins to complete the brim of your hat.

Acid rain

Splashing in the rain can be fun! But did you know that a certain kind of rain is dangerous? This is acid rain. It can poison water, plants, and animals, and even damage stone buildings.

Pollution

Acid rain is a type of pollution. It comes from the harmful gases created by burning fossil fuels, such as coal, gas, and oil. When the gases rise into the air, they mix with sunlight and water in the clouds, turning them into acid. The acid then falls as rain.

Acid damage

The Parthenon in Greece and the Taj Mahal in India are two world-famous buildings slowly being dissolved by acid rain. In Germany, acid rain has destroyed large areas of forests. Thousands of lakes in Sweden and North America are so acidic that the fish in them have died. The wind can blow acid rain clouds from one country to another. Pollution from industries in Britain is carried to Norway and Sweden.

Count the cost

Some factory owners say that cleaning up the gases that cause acid rain would cost them too much money. We burn fossil fuels to make electricity, but electricity can also be made from other sources, such as nuclear energy, water, wind, and solar power. These energy sources, however, are expensive to develop and produce. The only way to make the change to safer energy sources is for governments to change their laws.

COLIN CUMMING/ ENVIRONMENTAL IMAGES

Weather

WHAT
YOU
NEED

paper

paintbrush

glue

straw

poster board

ink

1 Place blobs of ink at the bottom of a piece of paper.

Blow the ink upwards using your straw. Be sure to blow out, not in.

2

3 Mount the picture onto poster board when dry.

You can create dramatic shapes with this technique

See how the lines look like dead trees

39

Spinning storms

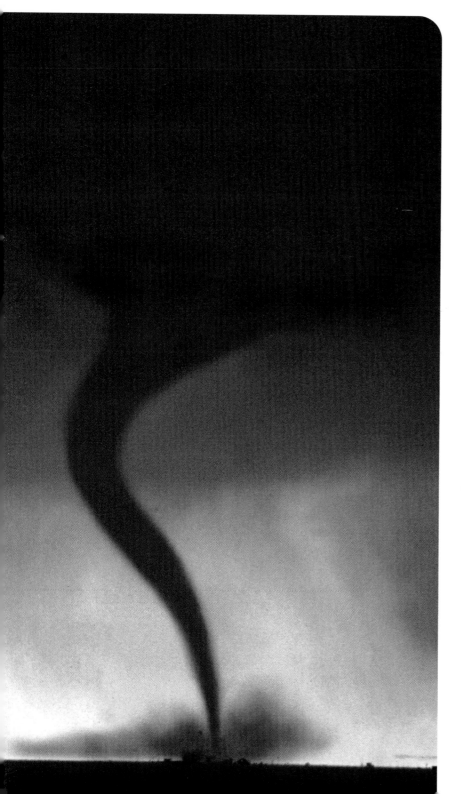

A hurricane is a gigantic circle of wind and rain. The winds of a hurricane can blow as hard as 200 miles per hour (322 km/h)! Tornadoes, or twisters, are only one hundredth as big as a hurricane. As they blow across the land, they can tear up big trees by the roots and push over whole buildings.

Super storm

Hurricanes start over tropical oceans. As great masses of warm, wet air rise, rain clouds form and begin to whirl. In the middle, the air is perfectly calm. This spot is called the eye of the hurricane. The spinning winds suck up large amounts of water vapor which later falls as torrential rain. Storms like this are also called typhoons or cyclones.

Air rush

A tornado looks like a huge, twisting snake hanging down from a cloud. Tornadoes start over the land when warm, moist air is underneath cold, dry air. As the warm air rises, it quickly cools, making hail and rain fall. Air rushes in from all around to take the place of the rising warm air, and begins to whirl. A tornado can blow as hard as a hurricane. As it travels across the ground, it makes a roaring sound. Powerful tornadoes can pick up everything in their path – people, animals, trucks, even trains and bridges!

WARREN FAIDLEY/ OXFORD SCIENTIFIC FILMS

Weather

Dizzy twister

WHAT YOU NEED

plastic bottle

black paint

newspaper

tape

wire and cable

bubble wrap

sequins

white tissue paper

glue

silver paint

bottle caps

1 Roll and twist pieces of newspaper and tape around the plastic bottle in a spiral shape.

2 Cover the whole of the structure with glue and finish off with a layer of white tissue paper. Leave to dry.

3 When dry, paint it black and then wrap and twist pieces of wire and cable around the twister.

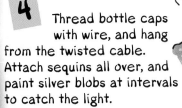

4 Thread bottle caps with wire, and hang from the twisted cable. Attach sequins all over, and paint silver blobs at intervals to catch the light.

Twisting, turning, spinning, shimmering. Amazing!

Turn your tornado around and around and listen to the whistling, clanking sound it makes. Just like the real thing!

41

Thick fog

L.WEST/ FLPA

Walking in **fog** is like walking through a cloud. Sometimes a fog is so thick that you cannot see very far ahead of you. At other times, it is like a misty veil. How thick or thin a fog is depends on how cold the air is, and how much water it can hold.

Smoky fog

Fog is caused when water vapor in the air condenses, or changes into tiny droplets of water. If the water vapor condenses around dust and smoke particles, it is called smog. Smog is most common in industrial areas, where factory smoke stacks belch chemicals into the air. Smog can affect people's eyes and breathing and is worse when there is no wind to blow it away.

Sea fog

When a foghorn blows in the night, it is warning other ships of coastal fog. Sea fogs happen in late spring, before the sea has a chance to warm up. When the wind carries warm, moist air over a cold sea, the warm air cools and condenses, causing a fog. The worst sea fogs happen near Newfoundland, Canada. Icebergs not only cause the fog, but are also an invisible danger to the ships!

Dew drops

Have you ever looked out the window in the morning and noticed the branches and spider webs glistening with dewdrops? This happens after a clear, still, autumn night when the ground loses heat quickly and there are no clouds to trap any warm air.

Weather

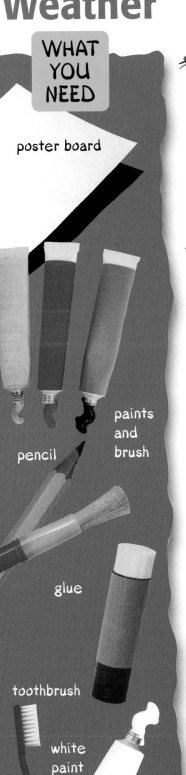

WHAT YOU NEED

poster board

pencil

paints and brush

glue

toothbrush

white paint

Foggy landscape

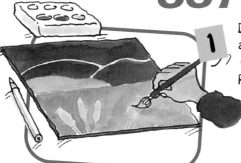

1 Draw and paint a landscape on black poster board.

Use the toothbrush to flick white paint onto the picture to look like fog.

2

3 Use your pencil to dot texture onto the picture.

4 Mount on white poster board.

Flick color on top of your picture to create a misty effect

Fly away home

When autumn comes, flocks of birds, such as geese, gather together to fly away. Have you ever wondered where they are flying to or, even more puzzling, how the birds find their way?

More food

Birds fly away, or migrate, from one country to another when the seasons change. Birds need a lot of food to keep warm, but food is harder to find when the seasons turn cold. As the days grow shorter, the birds have less time to search for food. So they fly south to a warmer place, where there is plenty to eat.

Magnetic force

How birds find their way, or navigate, is a mystery. Some birds follow the invisible **magnetic force lines** around the Earth. Others navigate by watching the position of the Sun. Night birds navigate by the position of certain stars.

Finding the way

A bird's **homing instinct** is extraordinary. Scientists moved a bird called a Manx shearwater 3,100 miles (5,000 km) from its nest, and set it free. Twelve days later it had flown the entire distance back to its home!

Long-distance butterflies

The monarch butterfly has one of the longest of all insect migrations. Monarch butterflies spend the winter in California or near Mexico City. In spring, they migrate north, reaching Canada by late summer. Then, they return south for the winter.

YOSSI ESHBOL/ FLPA

Weather

WHAT YOU NEED

paper

poster board

pencil

glue

scissors

tissue paper

cardboard

sequins

black paint

paints and brush

How many butterflies can you stick on your tree?

1 Draw an outline of a tree on the cardboard, paint it, then cut it out.

2 Cut leaf shapes from colored tissue paper and glue to the branches of the tree.

3 Draw and cut butterfly shapes out of paper. Paint and decorate with sequins. Glue them onto the tree.

4 Cut a triangular shape from cardboard as shown and glue to the back of the tree to stand it upright.

Birds on a wire

Draw an outline of birds sitting on a wire. Paint them black. Mount on poster board.

45

Glossary

air current A moving flow of air.

air mass A very large body of air.

air pressure The pushing force of air.

Arctic region The area around the North Pole where the land and sea are covered with ice.

atmosphere The mixture of gases surrounding the Earth that we call air.

barometer An instrument that measures air pressure, used to forecast the weather.

burrow An animal's underground home.

CFCs Chemicals that attack the ozone layer, found in some packing material, and sprays.

cirrus A streaky cloud that promises dry weather.

climate The pattern of weather in an area.

cloud Billions of tiny, floating water droplets gathered together in the sky.

cumulonimbus Heavy storm clouds.

cumulus A large fluffy cloud which promises warm windy weather.

drought A time when no rain falls and wells, rivers, lakes, and reservoirs dry up.

electric charge The electricity in something, such as a water droplet in a cloud.

evaporate To change from a liquid, such as water, into an invisible, floating gas.

fog Water vapor in the air that has changed into tiny water droplets.

frost Water droplets in the air that have frozen into ice crystals.

gale A very strong wind that blows at more than 32 miles per hour (51 km/h).

hail Frozen raindrops made from ice layers, called hail stones, falling from the sky.

halo A thin white light around the rim of the Moon.

homing instinct The natural desire of an animal to return to its home.

humidity The amount of water, or moisture, that is in the air.

light waves Invisible, flowing streams of light, also called light rays.

lightning A flash of bright light that happens during a thunderstorm.

magnetic force lines Lines of magnetic force that are part of the magnetic field surrounding Earth.

optical illusion A trick of light that fools your eye into seeing an image that is not actually there.

ozone layer The high layer of the atmosphere which protects Earth from the Sun's harmful ultraviolet rays.

power station A place where different kinds of energy or fuel are used to make electricity, or another form of power.

prevailing wind A certain wind that blows all the time, such as the trade winds that blow east to west across the Earth.

rain Droplets in a cloud which have grown too heavy to float in the air, so fall to the ground.

rainbow The arc of colors you see in the sky, caused when raindrops split sunlight into the seven colors of the spectrum.

reflection The image you see when the light waves from an object bounce off another surface before coming into your eyes.

shock wave A change in air pressure that results in a loud noise.

solar cells The light-collecting parts of machines, such as a calculator or a car, which work using solar energy.

solar energy The Sun's heat and light, which can be used to make energy, such as electricity.

solar panels Flat panels especially designed to collect the heat from the Sun.

spectrum The seven colors of light we can see.

stratus High streaky cloud.

temperature How warm or cold the air is, measured in degrees.

thunder The booming sound you hear during a thunderstorm. It is a shock wave, caused by lightning heating up the air very fast.

trade winds Winds blowing continuously over the oceans around the equator.

turbine A machine turned by energy. As it spins, it turns a generator, to create electricity.

ultraviolet rays Ultraviolet rays are part of the electromagnetic spectrum. Strong ultraviolet rays can damage plants and animals. Ultraviolet rays from the sun can also be harmful to humans.

water cycle The way in which water moves around the Earth. It evaporates from seas and rivers, rises into the air to form clouds, then falls back to Earth again as rain.

waterspout A tornado or whirlwind over water.

water vapor The invisible gas that forms when water warms up and evaporates.

weather balloon An air balloon that is sent into the atmosphere to measure temperature, humidity and wind speed.

weather forecast A description of the weather to come, usually made by a scientist called a meteorologist.

weather satellite A space satellite that sends pictures of weather around the world to computers on Earth.

weather station A place where information from weather balloons and satellites is received.

white light Ordinary daylight made of the seven colors of the spectrum, but which looks as if it has no color at all.

whiteout When there is so much snow, that you cannot see anything in the distance.

wind Air that is moving around the Earth.

Index

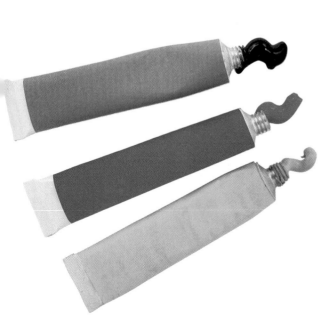

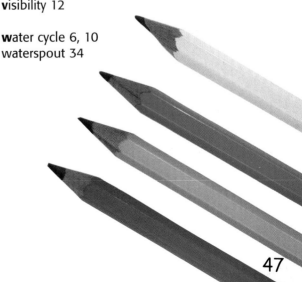

47

Materials guide

A list of materials, how to use them, and suitable alternatives

The crafts in this book require the use of materials and products that are easily purchased in craft stores. If you cannot locate some materials, you can substitute other materials with those we have listed here, or use your imagination to make the craft with what you have on hand.

Gold foil: can be found in craft stores. It is very delicate and sometimes tears.

Silver foil: can be found in craft stores. It is very delicate, soft and sometimes tears. For some crafts, tin or aluminum foil can be substituted. Aluminum foil is a less delicate material and makes a harder finished craft.

PVA glue: commonly called polyvinyl acetate. It is a modeling glue that creates a type of varnish when mixed with water. It is also used as a strong glue. In some crafts, other strong glues can be substituted, and used as an adhesive, but not as a varnish.

Filler paste: sometimes called plaster of Paris. It is a paste that hardens when it dries. It can be purchased at craft and hardware stores.

Paste: a paste of 1/2 cup flour, one tablespoon of salt and one cup of warm water can be made to paste strips of newspaper as in a papier mâché craft. Alternatively, wallpaper paste can be purchased and mixed as per directions on the package.

Cellophane: a clear or colored plastic material. Acetate can also be used in crafts that call for this material. Acetate is a clear, or colored, thin plastic that can be found in craft stores.

WHAT YOU NEED

gold foil

silver foil

filler paste

PVA glue

flour

salt

cellophane or acetate

   1 2 3 4 5 6 7 8 9 0   Printed in the USA   0 9 8 7 6 5 4 3 2